The Romance Book

SUMMERSDALE

Summersdale Publishers Ltd
46 West Street
Chichester
West Sussex
PO19 1RP
UK

Printed and bound in Great Britain

ISBN 184024 053 9

Jacket by Java Jive Design, Chichester.

Acknowledgements

Letters still in copyright are taken from the following sources and reprinted by the kind permission of the following publishers, individuals and organisations:

Everyman Library (p.103) from *The Paston Letters*

A. P. Watt Ltd on behalf of Sophie Partridge and the Garnet Estate (p.113) *Carrington - Letters and Extracts from her Diary*

John Murray (p.111) from a letter by Byron.

Contents

Romanticism is the art of presenting people with the Literary works which are capable of affording them the greatest possible pleasure, in the present state of their customs and beliefs.

Henri Beyle called Stendhal

Romantic Verse

How do I love thee? Let me count the ways,
I love thee to the depth and breadth and height,
My soul can reach, when feeling out of sight
For the ends of being and ideal Grace.
I love thee to the level of every day's
Most quiet need, by sun and candlelight.
I love thee freely, as men strive for Right;
I love thee purely, as they turn from praise;
I love thee with passion put to use
In my old griefs, and with my childhood's faith.
I love thee with a love I seemed to lose
With my lost saints,- I love thee with breadth,
Smiles, tears, of all my life! - and, if God choose,
I shall love thee better after death.

Elizabeth Barrett Browning

If ever two were one, then surely we.
If ever man were lov'd by wife, then thee;
If ever wife was happy in a man,
Compare with me ye women if you can.
I prize thy love more than whole mines of Gold,
Or all the riches that the east doth hold.
My love is such that rivers cannot quench,
Nor ought but love from thee, give recompense.
Thy love is such I can no way repay,
The heavens reward thee manifold repay.
Then while we live, in love let's so persevere,
That when we live no more, we may live ever.

Ann Bradstreet

She walks in beauty, like the night
Of cloudless climes and starry skies,
And all that's best of dark and bright
Meet in her aspect and her eyes;
Thus mellow'd to that tender light
Which heaven and gaudy day denies.

Lord Byron

Though weary, love is not tired;
Though pressed, it is not straitened;
Though alarmed, it is not confounded,
Love securely passes through all.

Thomas A. Kempis

All love, at first, like generous wine,
Ferments and frets until 'tis fine,
But, when 'tis settled on the lee,
And from th' impurer matter free,
Becomes the richer still the older,
And proves the pleasanter the colder.

Samuel Butler

Deare, when I from thee am gone,
Gone are all my joyes at once;
I loved thee, and thee alone,
In whose love I joyed once.
And although your sights I leave,
Sight wherein my joyes do lie,
Till that death do sense bereave,
Never shall affection die.

John Dowland

Through all Eternity to thee
A joyful song I'll raise,
For oh! Eternity's too short
To utter all thy Praise.

Joseph Addison

Never so happily in one
Did heaven and earth combine;
And yet 'tis flesh and blood alone
That makes her so divine.

Thomas D'Urfey

O, my luve's like a red red rose
That's newly sprung in June:
O my luve's like a melodie
That's sweetly played in tune.

Robert Burns

I love thee, I love thee,
'Tis all that I can say;
It is my vision in the night,
My dreaming in the day.

Thomas Hood

What's in a name? that which we call a rose
By any other name would smell as sweet;
So Romeo would, were he not Romeo called.

William Shakespeare

Romantic Prose

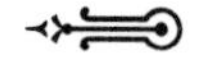

The way you let your hand rest in mine, my bewitching sweetheart, fills me with happiness. It is the perfection of confiding love. Everything you do, the little unconscious things in particular, charms me and increases my sense of nearness to you, identification with you, till my heart is overflowing.

Woodrow Wilson

I cannot exist without you - I am forgetful of everything but seeing you again - my life seems to stop there - I see no further. You have absorb'd me. I have a sensation at the present moment as though I were dissolving - I have been astonished that men could die martyrs for religion - I have shudder'd at it - I shudder no more - I could be martyr'd for my religion - Love is my religion - I could die for that - I could die for you. My creed is Love and you are its only tenet - You have ravish'd me away by a power I cannot resist.

John Keats

Love is ... born with the pleasure of looking at each other, it is fed with the necessity of seeing each other, it is concluded with the impossibility of separation.

Jose Marti Y Perez

He seemed to be gathering her into himself, her warmth, her softness, her adorable weight, drinking in the suffusion of her physical being, avidly. He lifted her, and seemed to pour her into himself, like wine into a cup.

How perfect and foreign he was - ah, how dangerous! Her soul thrilled with complete knowledge. This was the glistening forbidden apple, this face of a man. She kissed him, putting her fingers over his face, his eyes, his nostrils, over his brows and his ears, to his neck, to know him, to gather him in by touch.

D. H. Lawrence

Imagine two cars of the same make heading towards each other and they're gonna crash, head-on. Well, it's like one of those scenes from a film - they're doing a hundred miles an hour, they both slam their brakes on the floor and they stop just in the nick of time with their bumpers almost touching but not quite.

John Lennon's account of his first meeting with Yoko Ono.

When she saw him, she felt a stab in her heart that persons who have never been dazed by love take for a metaphor.

Abel Hermant

The ideal story is that of two people who go into love step by step, with a fluttered consciousness, like a pair of children venturing together into a dark room.

Robert Louis Stevenson

The best and most beautiful things in the world cannot be seen or even touched. They must be felt by the heart.

Helen Keller

Romance cannot be put into quantity production - the moment love becomes casual, it becomes commonplace.

F. L. Allen

Falling in love had changed the landscape of her life, as an earthquake did.

Charlotte Lamb

So he was happy without a care in the world. A meal together, a walk along the highroad in the evening, a way she had of putting her hand to her hair, the sight of her straw hat hanging on the window latch, a great many things besides in which Charles had never thought to find pleasure, now made up the tenor of his happiness.

Gustave Flaubert

Love does not consist in gazing at each other but in looking in the same direction.

Antoine de Saint-Exupery

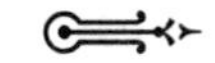

There are times when love seems to be over...[but] these desert times are simply the way to the next oasis which is far more lush and beautiful after the desert crossing.

Madeleine L'Engle

I think we have come out on the other side meaning that we love each other more than we ever did when we loved each other most.

Archibald MacLeish on 60 years of marriage.

Love is a desire that comes straight from the heart with a wealth of exceeding pleasure. Our eyes first give birth to love, and our hearts give it sustenance.

Jacopo da Lentino

Romantic One-liners

All love is sweet, given or returned.

Percy Bysshe Shelley

Love distils desire upon the eyes, love brings bewitching grace into the heart.

Euripides

Two souls with but a single thought, two hearts that beat as one.

John Keats

There is only one happiness in life, to love and be loved.

George Sand

Love is but the discovery of ourselves in others, and the delight of recognition.

Alexander Smith

Love is the beauty of the soul.

St. Augustine

What I do and what I dream include thee, as the wine must taste of its own grapes.

Elizabeth Barrett Browning

But to see her was to love her, love but her, and love her forever.

Robert Burns

When love reigns the impossible may be attained.

Indian proverb

To love is to receive a glimpse of heaven.

Karen Sunde

A life without love is like a year without summer.

Swedish proverb

Love is a beautiful dream.

William Sharpe

All mankind love a lover.

Ralph Waldo Emerson

A caress is better than a career.

Elisabeth Marburg

Each moment of a happy lover's hour
is worth an age of dull and common life.

Aphra Behn

There is no heaven like mutual love.

George Granville

Talking of love is making it.

W. G. Benham

The quarrels of lovers are the renewal of love.

Terence

Love can turn the cottage into a golden palace.

German proverb

When the heart clings to a lover, who cares what caste he be?

Indian Proverb

When two hearts are one, even the king cannot separate them.

Turkish proverb

Love conquers all things: Let us too give in to love.

Virgil

With you I should love to live, with you be ready to die.

Horace

Many waters cannot quench love, neither can the floods drown it.

Song of Solomon

Love cometh like sunshine after rain.

William Shakespeare

Love is never having to say you're sorry.

Erich Segal *Love Story*

No cord nor cable can so forcibly draw, or hold so fast, as love can do with a twined thread.

Robert Burton

Oh, what a dear ravishing thing is the beginning of an amour!

Aphra Behn

No, there's nothing half so sweet in life as love's young dream.

Thomas Moore

Love doesn't just lay there, like a stone, it has to be made, like bread; re-made all the time, made new.

Ursula K. Leguin

A noble hunger, long unsatisfied, met at last its proper food.

C. S. Lewis on falling in love

Love looks not with eyes, but with the mind.

William Shakespeare

Love must blossom. Through love will grow the trees and the bushes.

Joost van der Vondel

There is a name hidden in the shadow of my soul, where I read it night and day and no other eye sees it.

Alphonse de Lamartine

Without love, I should be spiritless.

Francois Maynard

You had my heart, and I yours; a heart for a heart, good fortune for good fortune.

Marcelline Desbordes-Valmore

Since we shall love each other, I shall be great and you shall be rich.

Victor Hugo

Your heart is mine; there I reign. I am content.

Pierre de Corneille

You are the prisoner of my heart; the key is lost.

Old German song

Love guides the stars towards each other, the world plan endures only through love.

J. C. F. von Schiller

One glance, one word from you gives more pleasure than all the wisdom of this world.

J. W. von Goethe

Love and the gentle heart are but the same thing.

Dante

Let your heart melt toward me, just as the ice that melts in spring leaves no trace of its chill.

Kokin Shu

How glamorous to die in love; how more glorious if the gods grant us enjoyment of one love; may I alone have enjoyment of mine!

Propertius

One kiss from rosy lips, and I fear no storm or rock!

Old German song

He who shall never be divided from me kissed my mouth all trembling.

Dante

Romantic Symbols

Fruit & Vegetables

Pear

A love symbol with erotic associations, probably due to its swelling shape, suggesting the female breast. The pear was associated with the goddesses Aphrodite and Hera.

Strawberry

This fruit is associated with carnal pleasure, especially in the paintings of Bosch, who shows giant fruit growing in his work 'The Garden of Earthly Delights' (c. 1495).

Fig

Both in the Bible and in art, fig leaves are used for covering male and female genitalia, hence the powerful sexual aspect to its symbolism. Another reason for the strength of its symbolism is that it was an important food source in the ancient world.

Bean

According to Egyptian, Greek and Roman tradition, a bean was a symbol of male fecundity and the promise of life to come. They were used as love charms in India.

Apple

The apple was widely used as a symbol for love, marriage, springtime, youth, fertility and longevity. The apple is also associated with the garden of Eden and man's fall from grace and is therefore a symbol immorality and temptation in Christian tradition.The 'apple of one's eye' is a person who is much-loved.

Orange

The orange is a symbol of love, fertility, splendour. Orange blossom was an ancient token of fertility used in bridal wreaths. The colour is associated with fire and luxury.

Tomato

The tomato plant native of western south America was named the 'Love apple' by the Spaniards. It was alleged to have aphrodisiac properties.

Flowers & Plants

Carnation

In Dutch painting the carnation is a symbol of betrothal, particularly when the flower is red. Pink carnations sometimes appear as emblems of maternal love in paintings of the Madonna and child.

Rose

The rose is a symbol of the heart and of sacred romantic and sensual love. The red rose symbolises passion, desire and voluptuous beauty. It is also a symbol of perfection and image of the cup of eternal life. Roman myth linked the red rose with the war-god Mars and his consort Venus (Aphrodite), and with her slain lover Adonis. According to a Greek version of the myth, Adonis was fatally attacked by a wild boar. As Aphrodite ran to her wounded lover she tore her foot on the thorns of a white rose, the drops of her blood turning it red.

Wild Pansy

Fable has it that the wild pansy (Love-in-Idleness) was originally white but was changed to purple by Cupid.

> Yet mark'd I where the bolt of Cupid fell,
> It fell upon a little western flower
> Before milk-white, now purple with love wound,
> And maidens call it, Love-in-Idleness.

Shakespeare, *A Midsummer Night's Dream*

Hawthorn

In classical times, hawthorn was linked to Hymen, the goddess of weddings. Its flowers were used in marriage garlands and the wood for marriage torches. This tree was also thought to protect chastity.

Myrtle

A symbol for sensual love, marital happiness, longevity and harmony. It is widely associated with love goddesses and rituals surrounding marriage and love. In China the crackling of leaves was thought to show whether a lover would be faithful.

Animals, Birds & Fish

Dove

The dove symbolises love, tenderness, peace, hope and purity. The dove was the attribute of the Semitic Love goddess Ashtart (Astarte), assimilated into the classical world as Aphrodite (Venus) and also Adonis, Dionysus and Eros (Cupid).

Partridge

The partridge is a symbol of love and feminine beauty. It was associated with the goddess Aphrodite and with grace and beauty in Indo-Iranian tradition: folk superstition crediting its flesh with aphrodisiac qualities.

Nightingale

The nightingale is a symbol of the anguish and ecstasy of love based on the beauty of the song poured forth by the nightingale cock during its spring mating season. The nightingale was said to sing of love, loss and yearning for paradise.

Duck

A sign of marital union, happiness and fidelity, this symbolism is centred on the Mandarin Duck of Asia, and was suggested by the synchronised swimming of the pairs. Duck motifs are used as emblems of union in the decoration of bridal chambers in China and Japan.

Deer

These are generally associated with virility and ardour, especially a stag with antlers. In art, a deer pierced by an arrow and with herbs in its mouth was a sign of lovesickness.

Fish

The remarkable fecundity of fish evoked the idea of rebirth in Medieval Times. The love goddesses of the Hittites were drawn holding a fish as their adornment.

Cowrie

Symbolic of female genitalia, the cowrie, especially the shell, was the natural amulet of sterility and the evil eye among many primitive peoples. It was used in charms in Africa due to associations with fecundity, sexual pleasure and good luck.

Jewels & Jewellery

Carbuncle, Garnet, Lapis Lazuli, Moonstone and Rubies are all symbolic of Passion and Love.

Ruby

The ruby is a symbol of ardent love. Its colour ranging from red to purple linked it with the fiery Ares (Mars) and Cronos (Saturn) who controlled passion. The ruby was said to inflame lovers and was believed to glow in the dark.

Lapis Lazuli

This deep blue stone is a love emblem in Greece, and was an attribute of Aphrodite, goddess of love.

Necklace

Associated with the idea of linking and binding, this is a symbol with sexual significance in some African cultures where the neck has erotic associations.

Wedding Ring

Why do we wear wedding rings on the wedding finger? The ancient Greeks and Romans believed that a nerve ran straight from that finger directly to the heart.

Other Romantic Symbols

Moon

It is a Buddhist symbol of beauty and serenity. The harvest moon (a full moon near the September equinox) is a fertility symbol associated with love and marriage.

Fountain

Cupid frequently presides over a fountain, which is a symbol of rejuvenating love. The spurting water is sexually symbolic, whereas a sealed fountain is a Christian image of virginity.

Plough

A male fertility symbol, sexual connotations were suggested as the male plough entered the female earth.

Triangle

An equilateral triangle sitting on its base was considered male. Sitting on its point, it became female. If drawn with the points touching, sexual union was symbolised.

Heart

Originally plainly drawn, this symbol gradually acquired Cupid's arrow, and it then became synonymous with Valentine's Day, a festival with pagan roots.

Liver

According to the Roman poet Horace, the liver was the seat of passions, and particularly of sensual love.

Lute

This was a popular emblem of the lover and also symbolised harmony in marriage. A lute drawn with a broken string denoted discord.

Food of Love

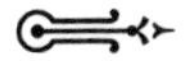

It must be a wonderful supper. We may not eat it, but it must be wonderful. And waiter, you see that moon? I want to see that moon in the champagne...

Henry Marshall, escorting Miriam Hopkins in *Trouble in Paradise* 1932.

Chocolate

The reputation of chocolate as an aphrodisiac goes back as far as the European conquest of Mexico.

In 1990, Herve Robert, a French doctor, discovered that the caffeine, theobromine, serotonin and phenylethylamine in chocolate make it a tonic, anti-depressive, and anti-stress agent, enhancing pleasurable activities, including making love.

Oysters

The connotations of female sexuality and reproduction associated with oysters are linked to their perceived likeness in form to the female genitalia.

For centuries, oysters have been thought to be an aphrodisiac. They are the highest known natural source of zinc, an essential mineral for human reproductive systems.

Rhinoceros Horn

The powdered horn of the rhinoceros is believed, in the Eastern world, to improve virility.

In China, the animal is a sign of good luck in romance. Mythologically, the rhinoceros was linked to the unicorn.

Ginseng

This is an Oriental virility symbol, seemingly based on the phallic shape sometimes taken by the growing roots.

Drugs made from ginseng have been used as reputed aphrodisiacs in China for centuries.

Honey

Honey was widely thought to have aphrodisiac properties in medieval times, although this may have been partly due to the effects of drinking mead.

In ancient times, it was considered the food of gods, seers and poets, whilst mead constituted the ambrosia of the Greek immortals.

Wine

Although not specifically an aphrodisiac, wine has long been associated with romance. The drink is linked particularly to a Greek God, Dionysus, which gives it ritual and magical connotations.

Herbs and Spices

Parsley and caraway are said to increase the desire for sex, while anise, basil, cinnamon, fennel, ginger, marjoram, rosemary and thyme are believed to bring love.

Lust, as well as love, is associated with cardamom, liquorice, vanilla and coriander.

Cloves

Cloves hold a special place amid the spices listed above. They were first used around 200 BC by the Chinese and were believed to have medicinal powers as well as being a powerful love food. They are the dried, closed buds of the tropical clove tree.

Champagne

Champagne has long been associated with love and celebration. It is allowed to ferment both before and after bottling, unlike wine, and it is the bubbles from the fermentation process that allow this drink to be absorbed quickly into the bloodstream, creating an almost instant effect!

Red Meat

This food contains high amounts of protein which floods the blood stream with the amino acid tyrosine. This in turn, triggers brain cells that enhance concentration and alertness. Libido is said to be thus enhanced.

Love Letters

'That's rather a sudden pull up, ain't it, Sammy?' inquired Mr Weller.
'Not a bit on it,' said Sam; 'she'll vish there wos more, and that's the great art o' letter writin'.'

Charles Dickens *Pickwick Papers*

Can no honest man have a prepo[sse]ssion for a fine woman, but he must run his head against an intrigue? Take a little of the tender witchcraft of Love, and add it to the generous, the honorable sentiments of manly friendship, and I know but one more friendly morsel, which few, few in any rank ever taste. Such a composition is like adding cream to the strawberries: it not only gives the fruit a more elegant richness, but has a peculiar deliciousness of its own.

Robert Burns to Clarinda (Agnes MacLehose), 21 December 1787.

You will understand that I should like to say many fine and striking things to you, but it is rather difficult, all at once, in this way. I regret this all the more as you are sufficiently great to inspire one with romantic dreams of becoming the confidant of your beautiful soul...

Marie Bashkirtseff to Guy de Maupassant, 1884.

If you only knew how much I love you, how essential you are to my life, you would not dare stay away for an instant, you would always remain pressed close to my heart, your soul to my soul.

Juliette Drouet to Victor Hugo, 1833.

My heart overflows with emotion and joy! I do not know what heavenly languor, what infinite pleasure permeates it and burns me up. It is as if I had never loved!!! Tell me whence these uncanny disturbances springs, these inexpressible foretastes of delight, these divine tremors of love.

Franz Liszt to Marie d'Agoult, 1834.

Dearest, - I wish I had the gift of making rhymes, for methinks there is poetry in my head and heart since I have been in love with you. You are a poem. You are a sort of sweet, simple, gay, pathetic ballad, which Nature is singing, sometimes with tears, sometimes with smiles, and sometimes intermingled smiles and tears.

Nathaniel Hawthorne to Sophie Hawthorne, 1839.

You fear, sometimes, I do not love you so much as you wish? My dear girl I love you ever and ever and without reserve. The more I have known you the more have I lov'd. In every way - even my jealousies have been agonies of love, in the hottest fit I ever had I would have died for you.

The last of your kisses was ever the sweetest; the last smile the brightest; the last movement the gracefullest. When you pass'd my window home yesterday, I was fill'd with as much admiration as if I had then seen you for the first time.

John Keats to Fanny Brawne, 1820.

So many contradictions, so many contrary movements are true, and can be explained in three words: I love you.

Julie de L'Espinasse to Hippolyte de Guibert, 1774.

I have not spent a day without loving you; I have not spent a night without embracing you; I have not so much as drunk a cup of tea without cursing the pride and ambition which force me to remain separated from the moving spirit of my life.

Napoleon Bonaparte to Josephine Bonaparte, 1796.

You know I would with pleasure give up all here and all beyond the grave for you, and in refraining from this, must my motives be misunderstood? I care not who knows this, what use is made of it - it is to you and you only that they are yourself.

I was and am yours freely and most entirely, to obey, to honour, love - and fly with you when, where, and how you yourself might and may determine.

Lord Byron to Lady Caroline Lamb, 1812.

Love does not lie only in gazing towards each other, but it is looking into our future together, with four eyes, I think this is the test of our love.

Gopal Puri to Kailash Puri, 1942.

You never knew, or never will know the very big and devastating love I had for you. How I adored every hair, every curl on your beard. How I devoured you whilst you read to me at night. How I loved the smell of your face in your sponge. Then the ivory skin on your hands, your voice, and your hat when I saw it coming along the top of the garden wall from the window.

(Dora) Carrington to Lytton Strachey, 1921.

No heart ever wished another more truly 'many happy returns'; or if 'happy returns' are not in our vocabulary then 'wise returns', wise and true and brave, which after all are the only 'happiness', as I conjecture, that we have any right to look for in this segment of Eternity that we are traversing together, thou and I. God bless thee, Darling; and know thou always, in spite of the chimeras and delusions that thou art dearer to me than any earthly creature.

Thomas Carlyle to Jane Welsh Carlyle, 1846.

It joys me to hear thy soul prospereth; the Lord increase His favours to thee more and more. The great good thy soul can wish is, That the Lord lift upon thee the light of His countenance, which is better than life. The Lord bless all thy good counsel and example to all those about thee, and hear all thy prayers, and accept thee always.

Oliver Cromwell to Elizabeth Cromwell, 1651.

To me you are the gate of paradise. For you I will renounce fame, creativity, everything. Fidelina, Fidelina - I long for you intensely and frightfully.

Frederic Chopin to Delphine Potocka, 1835.

Romance in Myth and Legend

Tristan and Iseult

Tristan loved Iseult of Ireland, although he already had a wife who resented their liaison. When he became ill, he sent for Iseult. The ship was to return from Ireland with black sails if she had refused to come, and with white sails if she was on board.

Tristan's wife, on seeing the ship with white sails, told him that the sails were black whereupon he died, thinking his love had deserted him. Hearing this, Iseult herself died of a broken heart.

Aset and Osiris

In Egyptian myth, Aset and Osiris were husband and wife, whilst both being fertility gods. Osiris taught his subjects respect and the laws of justice, while Aset taught the women about marriage, medicine and domesticity.

When Osiris was drowned by a jealous brother, Aset was able to impregnate herself with the last semen in his body, and although she failed to bring her husband back to life, she later gave birth to their son, Horus.

Rinaldo and Armida

From Tasso's *Geruslemme Liberata,* we learn that on the advice of Satan, the Saracens sent Armida to ensnare the young Christian leader, Rinaldo. However, Satan's plan was thwarted when Armida fell desperately in love with Rinaldo, and transported him to an enchanted palace where they whiled away the hours in each others' arms.

Freyja and Od

Freyja was a goddess of sexual desire in Nordic legend. She married Od, god of sunshine. One day he vanished, and she wept tears of gold, that were in fact corn-seeds, which covered the floors of her home.

Hathor and Horus

Emanating from Egyptian legend, Hathor took the form of a cow. When she married Horus, her milk was the food of the gods, which in turn guaranteed them fertility and prosperity.

When Horus lost both his eyes in a duel, Hathor was able to restore his sight. His opponent, Set, then abducted Hathor, and carried her off to his palace of darkness, from where Horus rescued her.

Angelica and Ruggiero

Ruggierio was a war hero from the Romantic epic *Orlando Furioso* (by Ariosto in C16th), who came upon the beautiful Angelica chained to a rock as a sacrifice, on the Island of Tears, where a terrifying seamonster lived. The tale tells of how Ruggierio overcame the monster using his magic shield and rescued the maiden.

Krishna and Radha

Krishna, having already broken many hearts in Indian legend, eventually fell for Radha. His love for her has inspired many fine paintings, in which the couple is usually shown in intimate conversation, sitting on a carpet of banana leaves, surrounded by birds and flowers.

For many Indians, Krishna is the one and only god and is an object of worship.

Paris and Oenone

In Greek legend, Oenone was a nymph of Mount Ida and Paris was the son of Priam, the King of Troy.

Paris deserted Oenone to be with Helen, and was then fatally wounded in a battle at Troy. Oenone had prophesied his disastrous trip to Greece and killed herself when she heard of his death.

Cimon and Efigenia

Cimon was purportedly one of several handsome brothers born to a wealthy family in Cyprus. He was uncultured despite efforts of family and friends to educate him. However, one day he came across the beautiful and refined Efigenia, asleep and near-naked.

He was overcome by love for her and resolved to make himself worthy of her. He learnt to read, to sing and mastered the arts of war. After numerous adventures Cimon finally won his bride.

Erzulie

The voodoo tradition of the Caribbean provides us with this goddess of love. When she is happy, she sends plenteous gifts and ecstasy. However, when she is sad, physical pain and other problems torment her worshippers. She is very unpredictable.

Bacchus and Ariadne

The Cretan Princess Ariadne helped Theseus to slay the Minatour and escape from the labyrinth belonging to her father, only to be abandoned by the man she loved on the island of Naxos.

Bacchus and his followers discovered the despairing Ariadne, and Bacchus was overcome by her beauty. He declared his love for her and offered her a place in the heavens amongst the stars.

Haumea

Haumea was a goddess of childbirth in Oceanic legend. There was no birth at the creation - instead, Haumea owned an orchard, with cows growing on the cow tree, dogs on the dog tree, etc. She herself grew leaves and one day, a leaf falling to the ground turned into a beautiful young man. She grew a vagina and made love to him.

When the young man eventually died, as leaves do, Haumea was heartbroken, and also died. However, she was reborn, grew leaves, and the whole cycle started again.

Orpheus and Eurydice

When Orpheus's wife, Eurydice was bitten by a snake and taken to the underworld, he was determined to win her back. He journeyed to the gates of Hades and pleaded with Pluto and Persephone to return Eurydice to him, but only for as long as a human lifetime. They agreed to let Orpheus take her back, on the condition that he did not look behind to see if she was following him until they had left the underworld.

Sadly, Orpheus weakened and turned around causing Eurydice to vanish from sight forever.

Mwambu and Sela

Originating from African legend, Mwambu and Sela were First Man and First Woman respectively. Their father, Wele, had created them so that the sun would have some people to shine for.

They lived with Wele in a Heaven-hut built on stilts to separate them from the earth. Wele let down a ladder so Mwambu and Sela could go down to earth and make a home of their own.

Omphale and Heracles

Heracles had been punished by the Gods and forced to be a slave for a year, and Omphale bought him at an auction. She made him dress as a woman and carry her parasol and Omphale began to wear his clothes, swaggering in tigerskins. They fell in love, and one day, while sleeping in a forest, Pan appeared. He had always lusted after Omphale so when he saw a woman's nightdress, he leapt on the person, only to discover that it was an angry Heracles.

Lif and Lifdrasir

According to Nordic legend, Lif (life) and his wife Lifdrasir (eager for life) are the only two humans who will survive Ragnarok, the end of this cycle of the universe.

They will either be sheltered in the leaves of Yggdrasil (the Tree of Life) or (in other accounts), be stored as seeds within the tree itself and will finally emerge and begin the human race anew.

Hero and Leander

According to the myth, Leander swam the Hellespont every evening to visit the beautiful Hero. Leander hailed from the Asiatic side of the water, whereas Hero was a priestess on the Greek side. It is reputed that Leander was guided only by a lantern that Hero held aloft to show him the way. Tragically, one night a storm blew up and extinguished the light, leaving Leander to drown.

When Leander's body was washed ashore, Hero threw herself in despair into the sea.

Romance in the Skies

At sunset you breathe the scent of lemon trees on the shore of a bay. At night, together on the terrace of your villa, with fingers intertwined, you gaze at the stars and make plans for the future.

Gustave Flaubert ***Madame Bovary***

Andromeda

A long constellation located east of Perseus and west of Pegasus.

In mythology, Andromeda, the beautiful daughter of Cepheus and Cassiopeia, was ordered to be exposed to a sea-monster as a sacrifice. Chained to a rock she awaited the arrival of the monster, but Perseus came across her in the nick of time, rescued her and slayed the monster. It is Andromeda's chain and the bones of the sea-monster which legend purports to be seen in the stars.

Hercules

This is a very distinctive collection owing to the 'flowerpot' shape made by four of its principal stars.

This is identified with the 'twelve labours' of Hercules. In classic mythology he was reputed to possess great strength and courage, and one of his feats was the destruction of the dragon which guarded the garden of Hesperides.

Ursa Major (The Great Bear)

Known alternatively as the Plough, the Dipper, Charles's Wain, the Chariot or Wagon or the Bier.

In Greek mythology the Great Bear is closely associated with the Little Bear and is connected with the story of the nymph Callisto, to whom Jupiter was over-attentive. Jupiter's wife, Juno, became jealous and transformed both Callisto and her son Acras into bears. Later Jupiter made them into constellations where he could watch over them.

Coma Berenices (Berenice's hair)

A small constellation appearing as a woolly collection of stars.

Berenice's hair relates to an old Middle Eastern legend. Berenice married her own brother Eurgetes, a King of Egypt. She vowed that if her husband returned safely from a war, she would dedicate her beautiful hair to Venus. When Eurgetes returned safely, Berenice, true to her promise, hung her tresses in the temple of Venus, but Jupiter was so enraptured that he immortalised them in the heavens for all to see thereafter.

Pisces

The twelfth zodiacal sign lies at the point where the path of the Sun crosses the equator at the beginning of the season of spring .

In mythology, Pisces is related to the classical tale of Venus and Cupid who were turned into fishes by Jupiter so they could escape the giant, Typhon. Maps depicting the two fishes show them with the tails tied together by a cord.

Virgo

Again located in the ecliptic, it contains the first-magnitude star Spica, and a large number of variable stars. Nebulas, over 500 of them, are a feature for which this constellation is famous. In ancient times, Virgo was known as a fertility or a harvest symbol and was usually represented as a maiden holding a sheaf of corn. This maiden represents Astraea, the goddess of justice, and daughter of Jupiter and Themis.

Camelopardus

This is a barren northern constellation, discovered in 1690.

It has romantic connections in that some historians believe it represents the camel who carried Rebecca to meet Isaac in the Bible story. Several of the apparently faint stars are in fact very remote, but extremely luminous.

Taurus

This very bright constellation is meant to represent the snow-white bull into which Jupiter had transformed himself when he wanted to carry off Europa, the daughter of the King of Crete. This area of the sky includes the reddish first-magnitude star Aldebaran.

Pleiades

This is a star cluster found within the constellation of Taurus. They are more commonly known as the Seven Sisters who, in Greek mythology, were being chased by the giant Orion. The God Zeus saved them by turning them into a flock of celestial doves, so that they could fly out of the giant's reach.

Hayades

Hayades is the name given to another cluster of stars within Taurus. They represent the daughters of Atlas and Aethra and were the half-sisters of the Pleiades. Entrusted by Zeus with the care of the infant Bacchus, they carried out this task very well and were rewarded with a place in the heavens.

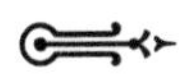

Romance in Your Stars

A horoscope shows the position of the sun, moon and planets in the sky at the moment of birth. There are 12 sections of the heavens, each ruled by a different sign of the zodiac. These sections are called 'houses' and the sun, moon and planets move through them.

The particular ruling sign and houses at birth, the mythological characteristics of the heavenly bodies, and the geometrical relationship between them can be used to predict events in the life of the individual concerned.

Aries

21 March - 19 April

Those born under Aries demand love and often take it for granted. Love is expected and accepted, but in many cases, an Aries does not understand how to return it.

The thought of being abandoned in love can bring on panic and terror, and continuous reassurance is the only thing that can calm these states of fear.

Taurus

20 April - 20 May

For a Taurean, love is synonymous with physical affection, which in a childlike way, is unquestioningly given and received.

Love is uncomplicated and appreciated, although many Taureans who have not yet learned its full value.

Gemini

21 May - 20 June

Geminis hold to the theory that there is more to life than love. They believe that love is still necessary, but may hold them back in life.

Men and women have not stopped desiring love, but they are prone to forget its warmth and safety and discard it entirely if it starts to become a barrier to freedom.

Cancer

21 June - 22 July

To the uncertain and sentimental Cancer, love is extremely important. However, in this case, love represents emotional security, a 'home'.

Cancerians' need for love is huge, although sometimes they try to disguise this behind tears and laughter.

Leo

23 July - 22 August

Love is a massive attraction for Leos, representing ultimate fulfilment. However, this can lead to being 'in love with love', whereupon they give love because they enjoy the gratitude and respect of the loved one. Leos do not like having to humble themselves for love, neither do they understand its true meaning or how to make sacrifices themselves.

Virgo

23 August - 22 September

Virgos are most at ease with a gentle devotion, and are often unwilling or unable to feel true passion.

Passion seems to consist of surrendering themselves, and that they refuse to do, so they channel any energy that love gives them into their work, always searching for excellence.

Libra

23 September - 22 October

Love is best along 'the middle of the road' for Librans; both the heart and the head are involved but it is neither detached nor passionate. However, Librans are so concerned with the surface beauty of love that they fail to understand it fully.
Librans do not question why they are in love, they merely recognise that they are in love.

Scorpio

23 October - 21 November

Love is a continual struggle for Scorpios. They are sexually uninhibited, yet at the same time, they are often mentally suspicious and rather fearful. This means that they are constantly trying to unite the physical and spiritual sides of love with a mixture of eroticism and purity. Sadly, this means that they are rarely satisfied.

Sagittarius

22 November - 21 December

In a desperate desire to discover true love, Sagittarians are constantly blinded by the idealism of love and therefore also constantly wounded by love's realities. They need to look within themselves, to their own hearts for love, because they will not find it in an idealistic insubstantiality.

Capricorn

22 December - 19 January

Capricorns have learned the important fact that love cannot be measured in excessive emotion. Love is quiet, and undemanding, a mutual gratification. However, it may be that they have not experienced true longing, due to the 'quiet' nature of their feelings.

Aquarius

20 January - 18 February

Love is an unselfish and rather detached emotion for this star sign, and is to be explored and enjoyed. Love's scope and dimensions are understood, but it is scattered carelessly and the feeling is often confused with friendship. The sense of fulfilment and 'oneness' is still just out of reach.

Pisces

19 February - 20 March

Unselfish submission defines love for the Piscean, who gains more pleasure from giving than from receiving. They often succumb to temptation and float from partner to partner. In this way, or by refusing any partners, they avoid becoming hooked by deep emotional commitment. Those who refuse both these directions and take a middle line are richly rewarded.